HOW TO DEVELOP A
POSITIVE
ATTITUDE

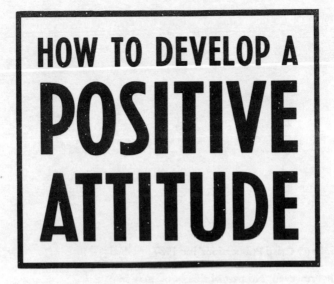

HOW TO DEVELOP A
POSITIVE
ATTITUDE

Elwood N Chapman

KOGAN
PAGE

Copyright © Crisp Publications Inc 1987

First published in the United States of America
in 1987 by Crisp Publications Inc, 95 First Street,
Los Altos, California 94022, USA

This edition first published in Great Britain in 1988
by Kogan Page Ltd, 120 Pentonville Road, London N1 9JN

Reprinted 1989, 1990, 1991

British Library Cataloguing in Publication Data
Chapman, Elwood N.
   How to develop a positive attitude.
   1. Self-actualization   2. Self-culture
   I. Title
   158′.1   BF637.S4

   ISBN 1-85091-548-2
   ISBN 1-85091-549-0 Pbk

Typeset by DP Photosetting, Aylesbury, Bucks
Printed and bound in Great Britain by
Biddles Ltd, Guildford and King's Lynn

CONTENTS

INTRODUCTION

The concept of attitude started to intrigue me 40 years ago while I was a student. Later, after becoming a professor, I developed a visual talk called 'Your Attitude Is Showing', and delivered it to hundreds of organisations during the next 30 years. In 1964, Science Research Associates Inc (now a subsidiary of IBM), published a book based on that talk, and now, almost a million copies later, the book is going into its fifth edition and is selling better than ever.

During this extended period, I developed some practical, commonsense observations about attitudes. I discovered, for example, that normal, successful, mentally healthy people, regardless of age or profession, are not automatically positive. These individuals (like the rest of us) continually search for ways to maintain and improve their positive attitude. Over the years, a few have told me that a positive attitude is their most priceless possession.

Questions such as 'What is an attitude?', 'Why are some people more negative than others?' and 'What can I do to help someone else become positive?' were common during my post-lecture discussions. The one question most often asked was, 'How can I stay positive?' This book will attempt to answer that question.

Although the views presented are not based on scientific research, I have attempted to the best of my ability to share answers to questions resulting from a half-century of observation.

For openers, my experience has taught me that attitude is a highly personal and sensitive topic. No one can force a change in your personal attitude. You alone have that responsibility, and you must do it 'in your own way'.

An excellent starting place in your quest to stay positive is to examine your present attitude. I suggest being honest but not too serious because too much introspection could cause you to lose your perspective and/or your sense of humour. This could be counter-productive as you work to develop a more positive attitude.

Elwood N Chapman

PART 1

Understanding Your Attitude

CHAPTER 1
What is a Positive Attitude?

On the surface, attitude is the way you communicate your mood to others. When you are optimistic and anticipate successful encounters, you transmit a positive attitude and people usually respond favourably. When you are pessimistic and expect the worst, your attitude is often negative, and people tend to avoid you. Inside your head, where it all starts, attitude is a mind-set. *It is the way you look at things mentally.*

Think of attitude as your mental focus on the outside world. Like using a camera, you can focus or set your mind on what appeals to you.* You can see situations as either opportunities or failures. A cold winter day as either beautiful or ugly. A departmental meeting as interesting or boring. Perception – the complicated process of viewing and interpreting your environment – is a mental phenomenon. It is within your power to concentrate on selected aspects of your environment and ignore others. Quite simply, you take the picture of life you want to take.

Emphasising the positive and diffusing the negative is like using a magnifying glass. You can place the glass over good news and feel better, or you can magnify bad news and make yourself miserable. Magnifying situations can become a habit. If you continually focus on difficult situations, the result will be exaggerated distortions of problems. A better approach might be to imagine you have binoculars. Use the magnifying end to view positive things, and reverse them (using the other end) whenever you encounter negative elements to make them appear smaller. Once you are able

---

* In reality our minds are aware of a variety of factors in our environment. For the purposes of this discussion, however, we will concentrate on a single, all-encompassing mind-set or attitude.

to alter your imagery to highlight the positive, you are on the right road.

Attitude is never static. It is an ongoing dynamic, sensitive, perceptual process. Unless you are on constant guard, negative factors can slip into your perspective. This will cause you to spend 'mind time' on difficulties rather than opportunities.

If negative factors stay around long enough, they will be reflected in your disposition. The positive is still there, but it has been overshadowed by the negative.

It is a challenge to push the negative factors to the outer perimeter of your thinking. Those who learn this 'trick' will reflect it, and others will notice.

Of course, no one can be positive all the time. Excessive optimism is not realistic. Friends and business associates will probably feel it is plastic. After all, a positive attitude is not an act: it must be genuine. Sometimes, when things get really tough, a positive attitude may be impossible, or even inappropriate. The 'we shall always overcome' perspective is more determination based upon rightful indignation than a positive attitude.

When things are going well a positive attitude becomes self-reinforcing and easy to maintain. Being human, however, ensures that something will always happen to test your positive mind-set. Some person or situation is always on the horizon to step on your attitude and challenge your ability to bounce back.

Winners are those who can regain their positive attitudes quickly. Individuals who are unable to bounce back, and who drag out or dwell excessively upon misfortune, miss out on much of what life has to offer.

The first thing Mary does when she wakes up each morning is to deliberately focus her mind on something positive – a sunrise or a special meeting with a friend. This gets her out of the 'right side of the bed'. She continues this practice throughout the day by actively seeking positive factors in her job, co-workers, friends. Because she is always looking for positive elements, she finds them. What she views (takes into her mind), reinforces her positive attitude. Mary is frequently asked: 'What makes you so cheerful?'

Mary's efforts to stay positive do not mean she ignores problems. It simply means she works to make the most of each day. She tries to solve problems as they surface, rather than allow them to weigh her down. *She knows that simply having a positive attitude will not solve her problems or make difficult decisions for her. She does not expect this to happen. A positive attitude does, however, put her into a better frame of mind to face problems.*

A positive outlook provides the courage to address a problem and take action to resolve it before it gets out of hand. Refusal to become angry or distraught can motivate you to assemble the facts, talk to others, determine your options and then come up with the best solution. Even if there is no ideal solution, your attitude can help you live with the problem more gracefully, which will help neutralise its negative impact.

> Although it wasn't easy, Tessa earned her degree while living at home with a stepfather who never accepted her. When asked how she managed to remain positive under such uncomfortable circumstances, Tessa replied: 'I made a sincere effort to be friendly and cooperative with my stepfather; but what got me through was focusing on a career goal that would earn my freedom.'

It may sound like an oversimplification to say you see what you want to see. Yet some individuals see the beauty in a wilderness; others do not. Some can turn a business problem into an opportunity. A few see the good in a child, friend, supervisor or situation that others cannot. To a considerable degree, the camera is in your hands, and you see what you decide to see.

The High Expectancy Success Theory works for many people. This idea states that the more you expect (attitude) from a situation, the more success you will achieve. It is a variation on the self-fulfilling prophecy, and the cornerstone of a best selling book *The Power of Positive Thinking* by Dr Norman Vincent Peale.

A batsman with expectation of success is more apt to score a century that one who bats only because his number is called. A job applicant who sincerely anticipates winning the position has a better chance than the person who simply goes through the motions.

The theory has a sound foundation. When you focus on the possibility of victory, your senses become sharper; enthusiasm is released and you come closer to reaching your potential. Modest expectancy does not produce the same results. The secret for successful athletes, salespeople, managers, and performing artists is the ability to combine high expectations with a quick recovery when setbacks occur. High expectations and an ability to bounce back are essential to success. One person defined success as the ability to get up one more time than we fall down.

Normally a positive person, Greg was thrown in a turmoil when his fiancée called off the engagement and turned to another. Instead of looking for the positive elements that were previously in sight, Greg saw only the negative. For weeks he wallowed in blue funk. Although he did not recognise it at the time, Greg was going through a painful, deep-seated attitude adjustment. The damage to his ego pushed his mind into a negative self-image and he became trapped. It was not until Greg became involved in some diversionary activities – a ski trip with an old friend, and a rigid exercise programme – that he was able to shift his mental attention back to more positive elements. Greg was able to regain his positive attitude without professional help (which in this case would have been justified).* He had won a difficult battle with his attitude and life became good again. His friends were glad he bounced back.

So what is a positive attitude?
A positive attitude is the outward manifestation of a mind that dwells primarily on positive matters. It is a mind-set tipped in favour of creative activity rather than boredom, joy over sadness, hope over futility. A positive attitude is that state of mind which can be maintained only through conscious effort. When something jars one's mental focus into a negative direction, those who are positive know that in order to bounce back *adjustments must be made!*

Summary

1. Your attitude is the disposition you transmit to others. It is also the way you see things mentally from the inside.
2. The more you can focus on the positive factors of your environment, the easier it will be to remain positive.

---

* The small cases in this book are not intended to portray serious cases of depression, where professional assistance is required, but only those with which we can all identify.

3. Everyone encounters outside events that can shake your attitude into a negative focus. When this happens and your attitude becomes negative, the challenge is quickly to employ an attitude adjustment technique that allows you to bounce back and regain a positive outlook.

CHAPTER 2
The Magic of a Positive Attitude

Using the word magic to emphasise the power of a positive attitude may seem like an overstatement. Yet if you have been a close observer of human behaviour, you have probably seen some attitude 'turn-arounds' that were so extraordinary and inexplicable that the word magic would be the only suitable adjective.

Read the following advantages of a positive attitude and indicate whether you agree or disagree by marking the appropriate square.

Advantage 1: A POSITIVE ATTITUDE TRIGGERS ENTHUSIASM

I've never read anything by a psychologist or psychiatrist that can clinically explain why it happens, but simple observation reveals that those who become negative and depressed lose much of their energy. They often drag themselves around as if they were in a fog. In contrast, when people are positive, their energy reservoirs appear to be endless.

Two months ago John had a bad experience at work. His manager bawled him out because an error surfaced on one of his projects. This embarrassment caused him to view his job with distaste. His long-term career goal suddenly seemed impossible. Although he had not made a costly mistake, John lost his self-confidence. His friends started avoiding him because he continued to dwell on his error.

In short, John allowed one negative experience to change his focus on life. Only 27 years of age and in excellent health, he plodded around the office languid, weary and 'burned out'. John's boss, who had forgotten about the incident, worried that John might be physically ill.

Today John is back on track and views his career with enthusiasm. His friends associate freely with him now that he is optimistic and self-confident. John's 'new energy' surfaced because his manager invited him to talk about what was wrong. This counselling helped John conclude that it was stupid to handicap himself with a negative attitude because of one mistake.

John's lack of enthusiasm was not due to illness, diet, hereditary factors or his environment. It was simply a negative view caused by a single incident at work. When John was able (with help), to adjust his focus, he automatically became more energetic. His reservoir of enthusiasm was there all the time – it just needed to be released.

AGREE ☐   DISAGREE ☐

Advantage 2: **A POSITIVE ATTITUDE ENHANCES CREATIVITY**

Being positive helps your mind to think freely. Ideas and solutions rise to the surface. A negative attitude, on the other hand, has a stifling effect and creativity is suffocated.

When Sue was employed by the advertising agency, everyone was impressed with her innovative ideas. Somehow, her imagination produced the right advertising idea for the clients at the right time. During the past month, however, Sue has been in the creative doldrums because a personal (non job-related) problem turned her focus negative. This situation has suppressed her creativity.

When Sue accepted her job, her positive attitude helped her to be creative. Today Sue desperately needs an attitude adjustment to regain her creativity.

AGREE ☐   DISAGREE ☐

Advantage 3: A POSITIVE ATTITUDE MAKES THE MOST OF ONE'S PERSONALITY

Many talented people – including those with desirable traits and characteristics – remain lonely and unhappy because they don't realise the importance of a positive attitude. They depend so heavily on their talent, intelligence, appearance, education, family or position to carry them that they forget that others enjoy being with people who are cheerful and optimistic.

Many people (including the author) feel that a positive attitude is the most powerful asset to any personality. This thesis can be found in the expression – 'a person with a positive attitude is twice beautiful'.

You may have noticed that sometimes a friend or co-worker suddenly seems more appealing without the benefit of factors such as a new hair style, different cosmetics or more stylish clothing. How could this happen? *A new mental outlook* by the individual could be responsible.

The foundation for the *Twice Beautiful Theory* is that a positive outlook helps eyes to sparkle more brightly, smiles to be more natural and engaging, and general countenance to be more vibrant.

AGREE ☐   DISAGREE ☐

To summarise, if you wish to make the most of your abilities and personality, it helps to control your diet, exercise regularly and pay close attention to your grooming. For the best results, however, it is more important to 'tune up' your attitude. This could be the magic that will 'turn on' your capabilities and personality and transmit your best features to others.

Summary

1. A positive attitude can provide higher energy levels, greater creativity, and an improved personality.
2. Other personal attributes become enhanced when you have a positive attitude.
3. A person not considered beautiful by physical standards, can still be regarded as 'beautiful' with a cheerful, positive outlook.

CHAPTER 3
Attitude and Career Success

In the work environment, as in your personal life, it is your attitude that makes the difference. Building and maintaining healthy relationships among superiors and co-workers is the key to success in any organisation. Nothing contributes more to this process than a positive attitude.

A positive attitude will expand your network. When positive, you transmit friendly signals. Customers, co-workers, and superiors are more open to you. Will Rogers' saying that 'a stranger is a friend I have yet to meet' is nothing more than attitude. Your attitude is expressed before you say a word. It shows in the way you look, stand, walk, and talk. If you are cheerful and upbeat, your attitude acts like a magnet. You not only attract others, but they are more friendly towards you because they sense in advance that you already like them.

Flora is a well trained registered nurse. Even more important, she is a therapeutic person to be around. Her co-workers and patients *feel better* when she is near them. Her warm, friendly attitude helps those around her to relax and feel better about themselves.

Flora's friend Liz is more reserved than Flora. She is unable to build relationships as easily or quickly. But Liz has several healthy long-term relationships because she knows how to *maintain* them better. Liz always spends time with others when they are 'down'. With her caring attitude she is always a 'friend in need'.

Ian has that rare skill of attracting new customers and co-workers as well as keeping old ones. As a result, he has used his human relations ability to build a highly successful career. When asked to comment on his competency he replied: 'Good human relations is the key to success and good human relations is 90 per cent attitude.'

Some individuals downgrade the importance of building and maintaining good human relations. They place so much emphasis on technical skills that they ignore the human issues. As a result they have difficulty in understanding why others often lack enthusiasm for their work although it is technically correct.

> Susan is a highly skilled technician. She always completes her assignments rapidly and her quality is among the best in the department. Unfortunately, Susan has a job that requires considerable interaction with others. She is intolerant of those who do not deliver the same quality of work that she produces, and is not reluctant to express this opinion. As a result, no one wants to work with her – and her supervisor is considering changing her assignment because her attitude has caused others to seek transfers to another department. Despite her talent, Susan is a victim of her poor human relation skills.

In the working world it is especially important to learn to separate relationships from personalities. A relationship is based on the psychological feeling between two people. Because you can't see or touch it, some people think only of the personalities involved. *They ignore the relationship itself.*

As a result, individuals often lose their objectivity. Instead of doing things to improve a business relationship, they get choosy about an individual's personality and a conflict develops. Those able to deal with the purpose of the relationship first are more apt to accept differences within another personality. By focusing on the job requirements, barriers can be overcome, which in turn will enable a better acceptance of co-workers.

Some people would rather find new relationships than repair old ones. In the workplace this can mean creating factions within a team, or switching jobs frequently. Those who want more from their careers recognise the importance of maintaining positive relationships. When a repair job is necessary, intelligent employees hasten to set things straight. They take this action whether they are responsible for the problem or not. Their attitude is that the relationship is more important than the incident that caused the damage. Working relationships, like others, are fragile and require constant care. Once neglected, it is difficult to return them to their previously healthy state.

Along with good work skills, career success depends on the quality of working relationships. An important first step is the development of a good attitude. If you don't *look for* the best in fellow workers you are less apt to find it. As a result, you will not become the kind of team player management expects. Your personal productivity may remain high but you will not be contributing as much as you could to the productivity of your organisation.

The well-known saying that 'no man is an island', is true. We all need other people. This is especially true in the workplace. Those who build a strong network of supporters create their own attitude reinforcement programme. It is difficult to remain positive without daily people contact. Co-workers, like personal friends and family members, can give your attitude the perspective, focus, and motivation to remain positive. Often it is possible to turn a day that starts off poorly into one that is bright, simply because a fellow employee is in a good mood. Attitudes truly are infectious.

Being positive at work provides a double dividend. First, it helps you to create healthy human relationships which lead not only to new friends, but also to career success. Second, any quality relationships you create provide reinforcement for your ongoing attitude needs.

Summary

1. Career success depends on both good work skills *and* human relations competencies. Building good human relationships must begin with a positive attitude.
2. Those who understand the importance of good human relationships – and are willing to initiate repairs when necessary – have a career advantage.
3. When a person is successful in building and maintaining positive working relationships a human support system is created that helps to keep that person's attitude positive.

CHAPTER 4
The Need for Attitude Renewal

Everyone – employees, students, homemakers, retirees – must occasionally engage in some form of attitude renewal or adjustment. There is no escape.

Renewal means to restore or refresh your view, rejuvenate your approach, re-establish your positive focus, and/or repair the damage of wear and tear to your attitude.

Weekends, holidays and short breaks are frequently used as 'pit stops' for attitude adjustment purposes. They are necessary to combat the following:

Environmental shock waves. As a seismograph records the intensity and duration of an earthquake, your attitude reflects tremors caused by financial reversals, personal disappointments, family problems, health concerns and so on. There is no way to insulate yourself fully from these shock waves.

Self-image problems. We frequently get tired of the way we look to ourselves. Maybe we have put on a few pounds – or are not as well groomed as in the past. This creates a negative self-image – a kind of dirty lens that keeps us from thinking of ourselves in a positive way. When this happens, working on a better image is mandatory. Health clubs, clothing stores, fashion boutiques, hairdressers and beauty shops are, in effect, attitude adjustment stations.

Negative drift. Nobody can explain why it happens, but sometimes, even when the environment is calm and you have a good self-image, there can be a movement toward a negative attitude. Some blame this drift on the negative aspects in today's society. The feeling is that because you are bombarded with so many negative stimuli through news stories, you tend to become more negative by association.

Regardless of the reason – environmental shock waves, self-image problems or negative drift – everyone needs to adjust their attitude on occasion. The rest of this book will give you ideas on how this can be accomplished.

Attitude renewal at the first level is a daily process. For some, a few moments of meditation may be the answer. Others, who seem to get off to a bad start, have learned to phone a friend mid-morning for a 'boost'. Still others use music or comedy as part of their daily routine.

Such minor adjustments happen any time, any place. 'Attitude adjustment hours' at the pub have become traditional. This ritual is strong testimony that some individuals feel the need for artificial stimulants to adjust their attitudes once the working day has ended. A few with serious problems don't wait until their working day is over. Many of these people eventually recognise that a less destructive and more permanent attitude adjustment is better for all concerned.

At the next level, attitude renewal can be a 'weekend project'.

'I use weekends for recreation. This helps to refresh my outlook so that on Monday morning I am rested and positive.'

'I find the quiet time during church each Sunday is a wonderful way to regroup for the week ahead.'

'Without weekends and the private time it affords me, I would be a burn-out candidate.'

Activities similar to those mentioned help many of us keep our equilibrium from week to week. There are times, however, when a major overhaul is necessary. Normal daily and weekend maintenance techniques are not sufficient when we find ourselves in serious attitudinal 'ruts'.

An attitudinal rut is when an individual follows a fixed pattern of negative behaviour for a period of time. Although some days are better than others, the focus seems permanently skewed to the negative side.

It is possible to be in such a rut without knowing it. When you become physically ill, for example, your body normally sends you a signal – you get a headache, a fever or a pain. This alert prompts you to do something about it. When you slip into an attitudinal rut, however, your mind may be unable to send you a signal, or you may refuse to receive it. Your friends may want to say something but hold back because they fear it might trigger an angry response. Or they send non-verbal signals which are ignored. As a consequence, some people stay in attitudinal ruts far longer than necessary.

> Over a year ago Don George fell into a negative rut when he was passed over for promotion. He had worked hard for it and felt he deserved it more than the person selected, Bill Stevens. Mr George is still negative. If you were to tell Mr George that his negative attitude showed, he would deny it. He has been in his rut so long he thinks his behaviour is normal.

The worst aspect of Mr George's situation is that attitude has a way of spilling over from work to personal lifestyle. This has made things extremely difficult for his family. This often happens.

If your job pushes you into a rut, it is likely you will extend it to your home. Correspondingly, if your personal life has negative effects, the chances are it will surface at work.

> Everyone at Hawthorne junior school wishes Mrs Bailey would retire. At one time students looked forward to her classes. Now they dread them. Once Mrs Bailey's colleagues enjoyed having lunch with her. They now avoid her. As far as anyone knows, nothing dramatic happened to cause Mrs Bailey to be in a negative rut. Apparently she simply drifted into it because of a lack of feedback. It is doubtful that she realises her negative attitude is so noticeable. She probably feels: 'I'm just getting older. I've been teaching too long.'

Mrs Bailey needs to learn that occasional adjustments are as necessary at 60 as they are at 16.

ATTITUDE ADJUSTMENT SCALE

Rate your current attitude. Read the statement and circle the number where you feel you belong. If you circle a 10, you are saying your attitude could not be better in this area; if you circle a 1, you are saying it could not be worse. Be honest.

	HIGH (Positive)	**LOW** (Negative)
1. If I were to guess, my feeling is that my boss would currently rate my attitude as a:	10 9 8 7 6 5 4 3 2 1	
2. Given the same chance, my co-workers and family would rate my attitude as a:	10 9 8 7 6 5 4 3 2 1	
3. Realistically, I would rate my current attitude as a:	10 9 8 7 6 5 4 3 2 1	
4. In dealing with others, I believe my effectiveness would rate a:	10 9 8 7 6 5 4 3 2 1	
5. My current creativity level is a:	10 9 8 7 6 5 4 3 2 1	
6. If there were a meter that could gauge my sense of humour I believe it would read close to a:	10 9 8 7 6 5 4 3 2 1	
7. My recent disposition – the patience and sensitivity I show to others – deserves a rating of:	10 9 8 7 6 5 4 3 2 1	
8. When it comes to not allowing little things to bother me, I deserve a:	10 9 8 7 6 5 4 3 2 1	
9. Based upon the number of compliments I have received lately, I deserve a:	10 9 8 7 6 5 4 3 2 1	
10. I would rate my enthusiams towards my job and life during the past few weeks as a:	10 9 8 7 6 5 4 3 2 1	

TOTAL _____

A score of 90 or over is a signal that your attitude is 'in tune' and no adjustments seem necessary; a score between 70 and 90 indicates that minor adjustments may help; a rating between 50 and 70 suggests a major adjustment; if you rated yourself below 50, a complete overhaul may be required.

Summary

1. Our attitude is constantly under pressure from shock waves, image problems, negative drift and other factors.
2. Attitude maintenance is a regular daily and weekly process everyone should engage in. Despite our best efforts, however, a major attitude renewal becomes necessary now and then.
3. It is important to know how much of an overhaul or tune-up may be required so that it can be intelligently planned.

PART 2

How to Adjust Your Attitude

The eight adjustment techniques in this section provide practical suggestions which can help you retain your positive attitude or, if necessary, restore it. It is recommended that you complete the exercises that go with each technique – *as you go!* In this way you can discover which techniques best fit your personal comfort zone.

ADJUSTMENT 1
Employ the Flipside Technique

The pivotal factor between being positive or negative is often a sense of humour. Attitude and humour have a symbiotic relationship. The more you learn to develop your sense of humour, the more positive you will become. The more positive you become, the better your sense of humour. It's a happy arrangement.

Some people successfully use the 'flipside technique' to maintain and enhance their sense of humour. When a 'negative' enters their lives, they immediately flip the problem over (like you would a gramophone record) and look for whatever humour may exist on the other side. When this is successful, these clever folk are able to minimise the negative impact the problem has on their positive attitude.

Jim was devasted when he walked into his flat. Everything was in a shambles, and he quickly discovered some valuable possessions were missing. After assessing the situation, Jim phoned Mary and said: 'I think I have worked out a way for us to take that holiday in Spain. I've just been robbed, but my home-owner's insurance is paid up. Why not come over and help me clean up while we plan a trip?

When the garage service manager handed Megan her repair bill, she was shocked and could hardly hold back the tears. As she got out her cheque book, she heard another customer say: 'Ouch! What a bill! I reckon my car doesn't love me any more. Oh well, no one said this love affair would be cheap.' Megan introduced herself; and later, after they became friends, she learned that Richard had the wonderful habit of 'flipping' bad news into something he could handle in a more humorous vein. It was a characteristic she learned to appreciate and imitate.

Humour in any form helps to resist negative forces. It can restore your perspective and help you to maintain a more balanced outlook on life.

How do you define a sense of humour?

A sense of humour is an attitudinal quality (mental focus) that encourages an individual to think about lighter aspects others may not see in the same situation. It is a philosophy that says: 'If you take life too seriously, it will pull you down. Most things aren't the end of the world and if you learn to laugh at the human predicament life is easier. When things get too tough, "bring on the clowns".'

In a classic mix-up, May found herself on a train travelling in the wrong direction. The mistake would mean arriving home for Christmas a day late. Upset at first, her sense of humour came to her rescue. Because of her positive attitude, she was given VIP treatment by the railway staff and she still enjoys the recognition attached to being called 'Wrong Way May'. The mix-up has become a favourite family story.

Cleo's sense of humour helped to turn a traumatic experience into a profitable one. Working late one night in her city office, Cleo became stuck in a lift. Rather than become negative by cursing her problem all night, she sat down, and laughed at what was an impossible situation. She even got some sleep before she was rescued early the following morning. Cleo recalls: 'Thanks to my sense of humour and a few prayers, I was able to accept the situation. After that experience, my company came to regard me as a person who could handle a difficult situation.'

Countless incidents, which you can improve with a humorous twist, occur several times each day in your life. Most will pass you by unless you train yourself to see them. To help you do this, it might help to give this mental set a special name. My nomination is 'funny focus'. It may sound frivolous, but it describes what some people actually do every day of their lives.

'Susan always adjusts more quickly because she has the ability to direct that strange mind of hers to the funny side.'

'Sam is good company because he can find humour in any situation.'

Those who receive such compliments nurture their 'funny focus' and thereby create a more positive perspective. This focus is their antidote to negative situations.

How can you improve your attitude through a greater sense of humour? How can you develop a 'funny focus' that will fall within your comfort zone? The following should help:

Humour is an inside job. It is not something that is natural for one person and unnatural for another. One individual is not blessed with a pot full of humour waiting to be served while another is left empty. A sense of humour can be created. With practice anyone can do it.

Laughter is therapeutic. Just as negative emotions such as tension, anger and stress can produce ulcers, headaches and high blood pressure, positive emotions such as laughter can relax nerves, improve digestion and help blood circulation. Dr William F Fry Jr, a psychiatrist and associate clinical professor at Stanford University Medical School maintains: 'Laughter gets the endocrine system going.' Of course, it is not appropriate to laugh away all serious problems; but any time you can laugh your way into a more positive focus it will help you cope with your problem.

A 'funny focus' can get you out of the problem and into a solution. Simply finding the humour in a situation won't solve a problem, but it can lead you in the right direction. Laughing can help transfer your focus from the problem to possible solutions. Using the flipside technique starts the process.

Why not give the flipside technique a try? You will discover that finding something humorous which you can share with others will cause your attitude to adjust faster.

To assist you to build this helpful habit, a special flip-side exercise follows.

FLIPSIDE EXERCISE

Most problems have a flip or humorous side. List in the circles below one or two negative situations to which you are currently adjusting. Examples might be a job change, new boss, or a different work schedule. Or it might be a financial matter such as a surprisingly high bill or an unexpected rent increase. Once accomplished, use the circles on the right side to identify any humour you might generate on the flipside. Keep in mind that if the technique was easy to employ, more people would do it.

SITUATION   **FLIPSIDE**

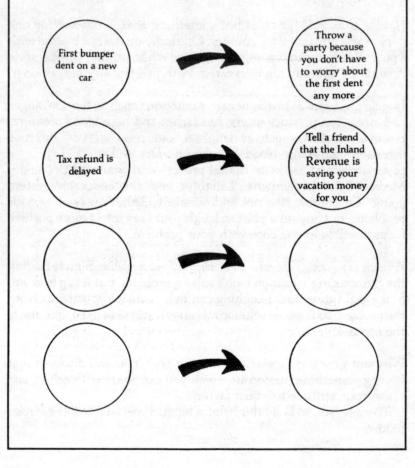

First bumper dent on a new car → Throw a party because you don't have to worry about the first dent any more

Tax refund is delayed → Tell a friend that the Inland Revenue is saving your vacation money for you

ADJUSTMENT 2
Play Your Winners

When retailers discover a certain item is a 'hot seller' they pour additional promotional money on to the product. Their motto is: 'Play the winners – don't go broke trying to promote the losers.'

This same approach can help you adjust and maintain a positive attitude. You have special winners in your life. *The more you focus on them the better.*

Julie has what she calls 'her special times'. Examples are listening to classical music, taking walks on the beach and enjoying good times over food with selected friends. Of course, Julie also has negative factors. Right now, she is bored with her job and is in the middle of a difficult human conflict with an ex-boyfriend. She manages to remain positive, however, because she has learned to play her winners.

Jack, at this point, has more losers than winners in his life. He is trying to lose weight; is deeply in debt and his car seems to live in the garage. Two positive factors in his life are his job (Jack is making progress in a career he loves) and running. By pouring his energies into his career and running five miles each day, Jack has not only been able to maintain a positive attitude, his weight is under control and he just got a rise. This happened because Jack knew how to play his winners.

All of us – at any stage in our lives – deal with both positive factors (winners) and negative factors (losers). If you are not alert, losers can push your winners to the background.

When this happens, it is possible to waste energy by dwelling on your misfortunes. Allowed to continue, your outlook will become increasingly negative, and your disposition will sour. Only you can change this. *Your challenge is to find ways to push the losers to the outer perimeter of your thinking.*

1. *THINK more about your winners.* The more you concentrate on the things you do well in life, the less time you will have to think about the negative. This means that because your negative factors receive less attention, it is not unusual for many to resolve themselves.

Gerald frequently keeps a daily diary about events in his life. He consciously stresses positives when making entries in his diary. As he falls asleep at night, he thinks about new entries he can make the next day. Gerald claims this technique helps him fall asleep faster, and gives him a better start the next day.

---

2. *TALK about your winners.* As long as you don't overdo it (or repeat yourself with the same person), the more you talk about the happy, exciting events in your life, the more important they will become for you. Those who drone on about the negatives of their situation do a disservice to their friends, and even worse, serve to perpetuate their own negative attitude. They play their losers over and over and wonder why they are not winning.

3. *REWARD yourself by enjoying your winners.* If you enjoy nature, drive somewhere and take a nature walk. If music is a positive influence, listen to your favourite record. If you enjoy sports, organise a game.

You play your winners every time you think or talk about them, but obviously the best thing is to enjoy them. If you are a golfer, playing 18 holes will do more for your attitude than simply thinking or talking about it.

PLAY YOUR WINNERS EXERCISE

List five positive factors in your life (include people, activities, or anything else that keeps you positive). Where possible, use a single word.

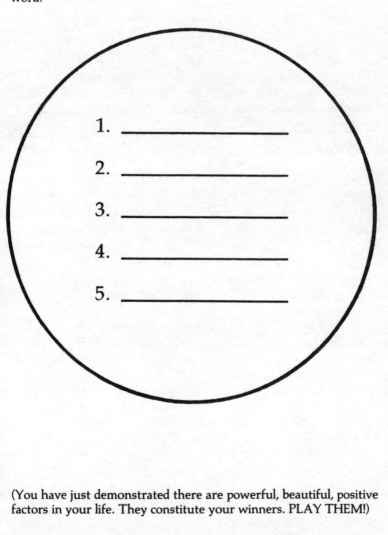

1. _____

2. _____

3. _____

4. _____

5. _____

(You have just demonstrated there are powerful, beautiful, positive factors in your life. They constitute your winners. PLAY THEM!)

ADJUSTMENT 3
Simplify! Simplify!

Some individuals unknowingly clutter their lives with negative factors which make it difficult for them to be positive. They surround themselves with unnecessary problem-producing posessions, people or commitments. Then they complain about the complexity of their lives.

The answer, of course, is to free yourself from complications. *Out of sight is out of mind.*

An uncluttered focus allows you to accept and enjoy life's simple pleasures. It is not distracted by a host of things that can drag you down.

To discover how you might adjust to simplify your life, read the following five 'clutter areas' and decide if any apply to you.

Clutter area 1: Unused and unappreciated possessions. Some otherwise sensible people become slaves to their possessions. They surround themselves with more tangible goods than they need or have time to enjoy.

Thanks to the success of Harry's electronic business, he and Glenda have a luxurious home which contains all sorts of appliances, gadgets, and electronic devices (including two personal computers). In addition they own a country cottage, two motorcycles and four cars. They seem to have an abundance of possessions to make them happy.
Unfortunately, they are so busy maintaining or worrying about their possessions that they don't take time to really enjoy them.

Almost everyone owns something they would be better off without. It could be an extra car that takes up space, or a boat that is expensive to maintain and seldom used, or a wardrobe full of clothes that are never worn. Getting rid of anything you don't need, use, appreciate or enjoy can simplify your life – and improve your attitude.

APPLIES TO ME ☐ DOES NOT APPLY TO ME ☐

Clutter Area 2: Too many involvements. Some nice people, in their desire to 'do good' and gain acceptance, over-extend themselves. As a result, they become slaves to business, social, or community organisations.

> Helen is so busy holding down a part-time job, working for her church, the PTA, and the Women's Institute that she has forgotten how to have a good time. If Helen could settle for doing a solid quality job for one or two organisations, she would not only receive greater recognition, but also simplify her life. This would definitely improve her attitude.

People who are generous with their time and talents sometimes don't realise that over-commitments can cause them to become hassled. Consequently their efforts become counter-productive.

APPLIES TO ME ☐ DOES NOT APPLY TO ME

Clutter Area 3: Career–home imbalance. Some misguided individuals devote so much time and energy to their careers, they leave their home life in shambles. These workaholics forget that an unhappy home life can influence their attitude and cause them to turn negative in the workplace.

> Sam is so committed to his career that everything at home receives second priority. Although he tries to catch up with repairs and chores at weekends, he never quite succeeds. As a result, he feels frustrated. Sam can't seem to see that by devoting more time to unclutter his home life he would help, not hurt, his career.

If people with both career and home commitments want a win-win situation, they need to do a good balancing act. This often means rearranging priorities so that both arenas are simplified.

APPLIES TO ME   DOES NOT APPLY TO ME

Clutter Area 4: Putting off the little things. Most people have the opportunity to 'throw out' many negatives that enter their lives, but procrastinate and keep these distractions around. Ultimately a build-up of minor negatives injures their outlook.

John suffered needlessly for three years with a foot problem that minor surgery eventually eliminated.

Jane put off having a simple repair done to her car until it became a major problem and ruined her attitude and bank balance at the same time.

Gary refused to take 30 minutes to fix a door that wouldn't close properly until it became a major irritant and caused a family fight.

Each life contains some minor unpleasant tasks. If they are eliminated quickly, they will not take a severe toll on one's attitude.

APPLIES TO ME   DOES NOT APPLY TO ME

Clutter Area 5: Holding on to worn-out relationships. It may sound harsh, but most of us may have a few 'friends' who have become negative and need to be eliminated from our daily lives.

Rita left her volunteer group and joined another, simply to get away from a person who was causing her to become negative.

Jim and Maria changed their caravan site location to avoid being next to a couple that were constantly fighting.

It is never easy; but, in some situations, it is necessary to terminate negative people–relationships to protect your attitude. This should be done quickly and without guilt. (It can be a more difficult matter when it comes to career or family relationships. In these cases, one must often be satisfied simply to insulate one's attitude against such negative forces. See Adjustment 4.)

APPLIES TO ME ☐   DOES NOT APPLY TO ME ☐

The flipside technique (Adjustment 1) will help you see more humour in situations. Playing your winners (Adjustment 2) will enhance the impact of positive factors and reduce the impact of the negative. Both of these adjustments can be quickly neutralised, however, if you clutter up your life with unimportant problems and trivia.

There is an extra dividend. Those successful at simplifying their lives find more beauty in it.

Simplify to beautify!

SIMPLIFICATION EXERCISE

Things I promise to do* to simplify my life.

1. _____

2. _____

3. _____

4. _____

5. _____

6. _____

7. _____

8. _____

9. _____

10. _____

* I will not procrastinate. I will not procrastinate. I will not procrastinate.

ADJUSTMENT 4
Insulate! Insulate!

It would be asking the impossible to think that all negative factors in our lives could be eliminated through any of the previous methods suggested in this book. Everyone, at some point, must learn to live with certain 'no-win' situations that cannot be easily solved, thrown out or ignored.

Almost everyone, including those with positive attitudes, have 'lived through' a period working for a difficult boss. Others have managed to stay positive in spite of a family problem that defies solution. Still others have found a way to cope in a positive manner despite an illness or handicap that is permanent.

What is the answer?

Work to insulate your focus against the negative factor. Employ techniques which isolate or detach these negatives so they cannot impact too strongly on your attitude. Find methods to push them to the outer perimeter of your focus in order to reduce them in size and keep them at bay.

The following list reveals adjustments people often make to keep a major negative under control. Think of them as Phase 1 insulators.

PHASE 1 INSULATORS

Keep busy
One day at a time philosophy
Play your winners
Exercise
Use humour
Simplify your life

> Concentrate on positive thoughts
> Do something for others
> Spend time with a friend

Long-term problems have a way of laying dormant for a while, then surfacing with a vengeance, causing the loss of a positive focus. Sometimes these problems will reach crisis proportions.

What adjustments can one make when serious problems flare up? The ways five different people learned to deal with such a situation are described below. View these as Phase 2 insulators that allow you to keep the problem in perspective while you work on ways to solve it or learn to cope with it.

Iris talks it out. Whenever Iris faces a recurring problem, she makes her attitude adjustment primarily through intimate discussions with close friends. Like letting air out of a balloon, she reduces the problem to size by getting it out of her system.

'I learned long ago that every so often I need to talk about my major problems to put them into perspective. It is sometimes hard on my friends, but I pay them back by listening when they need to talk.'

Jack works it out. You can always tell when Jack is dealing with a big problem by the intensity of his activities.

'Work has always been therapeutic for me. When I am faced with a difficult situation that seems to defy solution, you'll find me cleaning out the garage, digging the garden or working overtime at the office. When I pour my energy into an unrelated job my problem seems to get smaller.'

Michelle laughs it out. To deal with her no-win problems, Michelle refuses to take anything very seriously. This approach – a kind of psychological immunity – seems to protect her positive attitude.

'I know it sounds crazy but, when I can't deal in a normal way with one of my problems, I do bizarre things like roller skating to work, or wearing a funny hat until I have made my adjustment. I joke around until the problem becomes more manageable.'

Adele shares her problem with God. Whenever one of Adele's permanent problems resurfaces, she resorts to prayer. If this doesn't reduce it to size, she seeks counsel with her minister.

> 'God and I are partners. I do His work as a mortal, and then call on Him when I need help. It is a wonderful arrangement that never fails.'

Justin changes his environment. When an 'old problem' starts to nag Justin, he goes to the country where he claims a new perspective is possible.

> 'I'm a get-away person when the going gets rough. A change of scene pulls my focus back to the positive side. Don't ask me why.'

When major problems start to upstage your positive attitude, Phase 1 techniques (page 47) are helpful, but sometimes these more drastic adjustments (Phase 2) are required.

PHASE 2 INSULATORS

Talk it out
Work it out
Laugh it out
Give problems to God
Change of environment
Other

Each individual should design her or his own attitude adjustment programme. What works for one person may not work for another. The following exercise may help.

INSULATION CHECKLIST

The suggestions below may help you insulate your attitude against negative factors for which you do not have an acceptable solution. Read the complete list and place the number 1 in the box opposite the suggestion you like best, number 2 in the box of the idea you like second best etc, and continue until the list has been prioritised.

☐ Refuse to assume responsibility for other people's problems.

☐ Play your winners. Concentrate on factors which are positive for you.

☐ Find ways not to worry about things beyond your control.

☐ Share your problems with God.

☐ Talk problems over with good friends or professional counsellors.

☐ Use the 'flipside' technique; keep things light.

☐ Keep busy; work out problems through physical activity.

☐ Make a temporary change in your environment – take a long drive or a mini-holiday.

☐ Do something to help others.

☐ Engage in a special leisure activity (hobby, sports, card games, running, hiking etc).

☐ Other: _____

_____

ADJUSTMENT 5
Give Your Positive Attitude to Others

When you are frustrated by the behaviour of others, you may be tempted to give them 'a piece of your mind'. This is understandable. It is a better policy, however, to give them 'a piece of your positive attitude'. When you do this, it allows others to adjust your attitude for you.

> Sharon asked Kathy to meet her for lunch because she needed a psychological lift. Kathy didn't feel like it, but she accepted and made a special effort to be outgoing. When the luncheon was over, Kathy had not only given Sharon a boost, she felt better herself. Both parties came out ahead.

When you give part of your positive attitude to others, you create a symbiotic relationship. The recipient feels better, but so do you. It is interesting but true that *you keep your positive attitude by giving it away*.

When it comes to giving your positive attitude to others, you can be generous and selfish at the same time.

> Mrs Lindsey is considered a master teacher. The primary reason is because she freely shares her positive attitude with students and colleagues. In return, students and fellow teachers are constantly reinforcing Mrs Lindsey's attitude with compliments, attention and hard work.
>
> Mr Trent is an outstanding office manager. He is also a tease. Every day he creates a little levity to balance the pressure of work. In sharing his good humour he is rewarded by a dedicated staff that work hard to deliver higher productivity because they appreciate the pleasant work environment.

Everyone has several opportunities each day to give their positive attitude to others. Taxi drivers who make their passengers laugh will increase their tips. Employees who give co-workers deserved compliments increase opportunities for more open communication. Home owners can often eliminate problems with neighbours by giving away their positive attitudes when they see them. Holiday makers can enhance their fun simply by being pleasant to fellow travellers. Opportunities abound. The results are best, however, when the giving is *hardest*.

> It had been a difficult Friday for Jane. Because of a long, dull staff meeting in the morning, she was behind in her work. Just as she was starting to catch up, the computer went down. Then her boss asked her to finish an unexpected project that needed to be mailed before the weekend. When she finally left work after 6 pm all Jane could think of was getting in her bath and forgetting it all. But she had promised to visit her friend, Jackie, who was in hospital. The temptation to drive straight home was strong, but she resisted and made her visit. Jackie appreciated it so much, that when Jane arrived home she was refreshed and positive. She didn't need the bath to make her feel better.

The less you feel like giving part of your positive attitude away, the more *giving it away* will do for you. Sometimes it can get you out of your own rut.

> Joe has been in a bad mood for weeks. Last night, discouraged with his present state of mind, he decided to do something nice for his sister who had been having a difficult time with her divorce. He phoned her on the spur of the moment and asked her to go climbing. After a great weekend, Joe returned with a positive outlook. Was it the change of environment, the fresh air, or the exercise that caused the change? Partially, but much of the improvement was helping Kathy regain her focus, too.

Everyone winds up a winner by sharing positive attitudes with others. The exercise that follows may help you decide which ways are best for you.

ATTITUDE GIVEAWAY EXERCISE

Different ways people share their positive attitudes are listed below. Some may appeal to you; others will not. Place a mark in the square opposite *three* that fit your style – and that you intend to incorporate into your behaviour.

 Going out of my way to visit friends who may be having trouble with *their* attitudes.

 Being more positive among those with whom I have daily contact.

 Transmitting my positive attitude to others whenever I use the telephone.

Sharing my positive attitude by sending token items such as cards or flowers to those I care about.

Sharing my sense of humour through more teasing, telling jokes or using the flipside technique.

 Being more sensitive as a listener so others can regain their positive focus.

 Laughing more, so that my attitude will be infectious and others will pick it up.

 Communicating my attitude through upbeat conversations, paying compliments to others etc.

Giving my attitude to others by setting a better example as a positive person.

As you implement your choices, remind yourself that the more you give your attitude away, the more positive it will remain.

ADJUSTMENT 6
Look Better to Yourself

We are constantly bombarded through advertising to improve our image. Most messages claim you will find acceptance and meet new friends with a 'new look'.

'Discover the new you. Join our health club and expand your circle of friends.'

'Let plastic surgery help you find a new partner.'

Self-improvement of any kind should be applauded, but the overriding reason for a 'new image' is not to look better for others; rather it should be because you want to look better to yourself. When you improve your appearance, you give your positive attitude a boost.

The term 'inferiority complex' is not in popular use today, but I still relish this old, textbook definition: *an inferiority complex is when you look better to others than you do to yourself*. In other words, when you have a negative self-image, you make yourself psychologically inferior.

The truth is that you often look better to others than you do to yourself. There may be periods when you feel unfashionable, unattractive or poorly groomed. This does not necessarily mean you look that way to your friends, but you end up communicating a negative attitude because you don't look good to yourself.

When you have a poor self-image, it is as though you are looking through a glass darkly. When you feel you don't look good, nothing else looks good to you.

When you look good to yourself, the world seems brighter. You are more in focus.

When my wife Martha and I were first married, she had her hair done each Friday. It was a ritual. Sometimes, when our budget was tight, I wasn't sure it was necessary. What I didn't realise at the time was how much it helped her outlook. Granted, it improved her appearance, but that was not the important thing. What was important was that Martha looked better to herself. It took me a while to realise that Friday was often our best day together.

Sometimes I think people might have better attitudes if mirrors had never been invented.

Clyde was a successful insurance agent. His most distinguishing feature was his bald head. Imagine my surprise when Clyde asked my opinion about his getting a hair piece. Knowing he was a scuba diver, my first thought was of Clyde losing his hair piece when he went swimming along a rocky coast. What I said however was: 'If the idea appeals to you, do it.' Clyde followed through. His 'new look' and more positive attitude made him more self-confident and ultimately more successful than ever.

You see yourself first, your environment second. You can't remove yourself from this perceptual process.

Cedric gave up on his self-image when he was a teenager. All through school he was considered a loner and a swat. Approaching final examinations, Cedric enrolled in a course designed to prepare students to find employment. Part of the programme included a mock employment interview on video tape which would be assessed by the instructor and fellow students. To prepare for this difficult ordeal, Cedric purchased a new suit, had his hair restyled and bought new, more fashionable spectacle frames. He practised over and over at home. When his day arrived, Cedric did so well he received compliments from all who viewed the tape. This recognition and support had a wonderful impact on him. For the first time, he looked good to himself. His negative image suddenly turned positive and was no longer a handicap to his future.

ADJUSTING YOUR POSITIVE ATTITUDE
THROUGH IMAGE IMPROVEMENT

Five general physical and psychological activities people engage in to improve or maintain their self-images are shown below. Draw a line through those that do not fit your personal comfort zone.

Wardrobe improvement. Pay more attention (and money, if necessary) to what you wear, how you coordinate various fashion items, colours etc. Make the best 'fashion statement' possible.

Hairstyle, cosmetics. Spend more time with your hairstyle, facial appearance etc.

Looking healthy. Devote time to an exercise programme: anything that will create a healthier appearance. Include posture, dental care, weight control, diet, more time in the open air etc.

Being yourself. Refuse to be over-influenced by others and the media. Stay with your own idea of what your image should be. Be different in the way *you* want to be different.

Image-attitude connection. Accept the premise that your attitude will suffer if you don't keep a good self-image. Even if you don't care about how others think you look, care about how you look to yourself because it is important to your own attitude.

If one or more of the five remain – and you make progress in that area – you can expect to become a more positive person.

The connection between a good self-image and a positive attitude cannot be ignored. In keeping a better image it will help if you: (1) Admit that at times you may look better to others than you look to yourself. (2) Play up your winning features – hair, smile, eyes etc. (3) Make improvements in grooming – when improvement is possible.

ADJUSTMENT 7
Accept the Physical Connection

Apparently no one has been able to prove conclusively a clinical relationship between physical well-being and attitude. Most, however, including the most cynical of researchers in the area, concede there is a connection. Please answer the following questions and compare your answers with those of the author.

PRE-TEST

True **False**

____ ____ 1. Exercise can do as much or more to adjust your attitude as a cocktail hour.

____ ____ 2. Following a good diet has nothing to do with improving your self-image.

____ ____ 3. The better you feel physically on a given day, the more positive your attitude is apt to be.

____ ____ 4. Neither a sense of physical well-being nor a positive attitude can be stored indefinitely.

____ ____ 5. Daily exercise can do little to keep one positive.

Author's answers: 1. T (both will change your focus, but exercise is better for you and lasts longer); 2. F; 3. T; 4. T; 5. F (daily exercise is an outstanding attitude adjuster).

More than at any previous time people are aware of physical fitness. A surprising number of us incorporate daily work-outs into our schedules. This commitment to the 'attitude connection' is expressed in these typical comments.

'My work-out does as much for my mental state as it does for my body.'

'Exercise tones up my body and tunes up my outlook.'

'I never underestimate what my daily work-out does for me psychologically.'

Many fitness enthusiasts depend upon exercise to keep them out of attitudinal ruts.

'I've renamed my health club the Attitude Adjustment Factory.'

'When I'm worried or depressed, I take a long walk. It has a way of pushing negative thoughts out of my system.'

'A tough work-out can get me out of a mental rut.'

No single group in our society deals more with the psychological aspects of attitude than professional athletes. Increasingly, athletes engage year round in sophisticated physical conditioning programmes. They realise they must stay in shape to remain competitive. If you listen carefully, coaches and managers talk more about attitude, however, than physical conditioning.

'We made the semi-finals this year because we have a new team attitude.'

'I owe my success this season to my coach. He helped me to adjust not only my technique, but more importantly my attitude.'

'My success this year is because of greater self-confidence. I finally began to believe in myself.'

Important as talent and physical conditioning are, most players, coaches and sportscasters talk about mental attitude as most important.

They must be trying to tell us something.

BALANCING EXERCISE

In my desire to become a more positive person, I recognise that I may need a better balance between mental adjustments and physical exercise. To achieve this goal, I intend to do the following.

List ATTITUDE ADJUSTMENTS you intend to employ.	My DAILY EXERCISE PROGRAMME in the future will consist of:

ADJUSTMENT 8
Clarify Your Mission

It has been my observation that an individual with a purpose is more apt to have a positive attitude than someone without direction. It need not be an all-consuming mission that reaches for the stars, but it should be sufficiently strong to provide a steady, ongoing challenge.

Mrs Payne lost her husband in a car accident when their two sons were babies. Since the accident, her primary purpose in life has been to do the best job possible raising her boys. Mrs Payne is so dedicated to her goal she refuses to allow herself negative attitudes.

Harry discovered he had musical talent while at school. Today, at 40, he works as an engineer during the day and plays piano in a local restaurant at night. Harry's dominant interest in life is his music. He is happiest when sharing his musical talents.

Emma spent years as an administrative clerk in a retail store. One day her boss asked her to fill in for a salesperson who phoned in to say she was ill. Emma enjoyed the new challenge so much she redirected her life towards sales. Today she is a senior buyer at the largest shop in town.

A mission in life provides direction, helps individuals achieve better focus, dissipates fears, provides perspective and destroys uncertainty.

Having direction gives a person a stronger grip on her or his attitude. The negative is easier to control.

Charlene has always liked nature. This interest has led her to a mission whereby she does everything possible to protect and preserve the beauty of her environment. As a teacher, Charlene teaches her students to respect all living creatures. She shares with them the beauty in everything that grows. Her purpose takes her beyond the classroom. She is an active member of a leading environmental group, and has had a number of nature articles published. Asked to state her activities in simple terms, Charlene said: 'I want to leave my environment more beautiful than when I arrived.'

It is difficult to picture Charlene without her mission. It provides her with recognition and identity, and a positive outlook on life.

Some people throw up their hands in despair when it comes to finding a primary purpose in life. They profess 'I don't want anything to control me. I don't need a special challenge. I just want to live day to day.' Many of these people may wonder, at times, why they are not getting more out of life.

MISSION EXERCISE

Searching for, or clarifying a life's purpose, can be fun. To assist you in this process, you are invited to answer this question.

WHAT WOULD BE YOUR PRIMARY GOAL IF YOU HAD ONE YEAR TO LIVE AND YOU WERE GUARANTEED SUCCESS IN WHATEVER YOU ATTEMPTED?

Answer the question by drawing or sketching a picture, design or symbol that represents your primary purpose. (Mrs Payne would probably sketch two children; Harry might draw some musical notes.)

Draw your design inside the circle without using a single word.

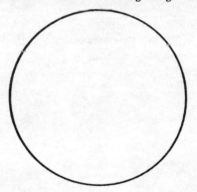

Whatever you draw could be your primary purpose in life. Think about ways you can help it become a reality.

Summary

Although all eight of the ATTITUDE ADJUSTMENT TECH-NIQUES can be used both to *maintain* and *restore* a positive attitude, some may be more effective at one than the other. If you feel one of the adjustment techniques is more effective helping you *maintain* a positive attitude, place an X in the appropriate column. If you feel a technique would be more effective in helping you *restore* a positive attitude, place an X in the second column. Should you feel a technique would be *equally* effective in both areas, place an X in both columns.

	MAINTAIN	RESTORE
1. Flipside Technique		
2. Play Your Winners		
3. Simplify! Simplify!		
4. Insulate! Insulate!		
5. Give Your Positive Attitude to Others		
6. Look Better to Yourself		
7. Accept the Physical Condition		
8. Clarify Your Life's Mission		

PART 3

Conclusion

Attitude and Leadership

More business successes are won on attitude than technical achievement. Managers who know how to build positive attitudes among their employees can lead less experienced teams to increased productivity and success. It happens all the time.

> Gloria, a manager in a medium-size company, uses three human relations techniques to develop positive attitudes with her employees: (1) she always provides positive recognition when earned; (2) she looks for something to compliment each employee on at least once each week; (3) she stays positive herself. Gloria never complains about the quality of her employees. She maintains a sense of humour which makes a rigorous assignment a positive experience. The combination of the three techniques creates a wave of confidence that the other departments notice. Other managers sometimes feel Gloria's human relations approach lacks toughness and discipline. After the results are in, however, it is difficult to defend this feeling.

This is not to say that developing specific skills is neglected. Gloria works through training to raise the performance of her employees as high as possible. She provides both group and individual instruction. Nor does Gloria's emphasis on a positive attitude mean that strategic planning is unimportant. It simply means that attitude is the glue that brings her team together – and turns it into a winner.

All managers, teachers and volunteer leaders are 'coaches'. How can you use leadership techniques to achieve greater productivity from your employees, students, or volunteers? Here are five principles you might consider. Please indicate whether you agree or disagree.

Agree	Disagree	The Rotten Apple Principle
☐	☐	Given enough time, one rotten apple in a barrel will spoil the rest. Given enough time, one negative team member will destroy the positive attitudes of the others. To resolve this means that the negative person should be counselled by the leader until he or she makes an attitude adjustment or other action is taken. In professional sports, for a highly talented player this can mean a transfer. In all cases, waiting too long can destroy productivity and the 'game is lost'.

Agree	Disagree	The Policy of Sound Human Relations
☐	☐	Sound human principles, such as treating each person as an individual using the Mutual Reward Principle, and being sensitive to the needs of others, should be honoured. Any leader who uses dehumanising techniques, such as bullying an individual in front of the team, can destroy morale.

Agree	Disagree	Attitudes are caught, not taught
☐	☐	This principle means that the attitudes of followers reflect the attitudes of their leader. The first responsibility of any leader is to maintain her or his own positive attitude. It might be a good idea to review the eight adjustment steps

presented in this book until they are
committed to memory.

Agree	Disagree	**The attitude/confidence connection**
☐	☐	This basic principle states that team members with positive outlooks enjoy greater personal confidence. Golfers without confidence never make the cut. Sales representatives without confidence might as well stay at home. Nurses without confidence do their patients a disservice. Supervisors without confidence are seldom successful. *The foundation for personal confidence is a positive outlook.*

Agree	Disagree	**The instant replay principle**
☐	☐	The process of attitude renewal (positive approach) should start whenever a problem is encountered.

Summary

1. In some roles (team building, selling, customer relations etc) attitude is more important than talent.
2. Leaders who follow certain attitude-building principles (ie attitudes are caught – not taught) are measurably more successful.
3. The process of attitude renewal should start immediately following a defeat or failure.

Protecting Your Most
Priceless Possession

An intriguing experiment would be to randomly select 100 people and (1) have each individual list all of his or her current problems on a sheet of paper, (2) place the sheets in a box and mix, (3) have the same people draw a sheet (not their own) from the box.

What would be learned?
Everybody would end up with a list of problems. Some participants would discover they have fewer and less serious problems than on the list they selected. This should help their attitude. Others would discover they had more severe problems, but realise that no one is immune to difficulties. If the experiment was taken one step further, something even more significant would become apparent. Namely, that some of those with the most severe problems would have the most positive attitudes.

What does this tell us?
It says that the number and severity of problems related to living conditions, financial status, amount of education, good/bad luck or physical well-being do not determine a person's attitude. Stated another way – *You have the capacity to be positive under all conceivable circumstances.*

This is true even when a new, major problem disrupts your life. Under these conditions, the *way* (attitude) you deal with the problem is decisive. The following three-step procedure might help.

Step 1: Slow down until you gain a positive perspective
Whenever a heavy problem arises, it is a good idea to back away to gain the best possible focus. Because this is difficult to do, some 'sleep on the problem', take a mini holiday or seek the advice of another

person. Such actions can produce an outlook more conducive to finding alternatives that could lead to a solution.

Step 2: Identify the best possible solution
This usually means engaging yourself in the traditional, scientific decision-making process. First, get all the facts. Next, isolate the alternatives. Then weigh them carefully to arrive at the best decision. Never an easy process, it is sometimes wise to use a professional counsellor as a resource and guide.

Step 3: Live with the solution gracefully
Not all solutions are ideal, but once a decision has been made, it deserves your best effort. This usually means regaining your previous perspective (attitude) so you do not continue to re-process the problem endlessly in your mind.

Next to serious or severe problems, few events can test a positive attitude more than making the adjustment to a new lifestyle change. Moving to a new part of the country, making a career change, or going through the transition into retirement can put your attitude 'through the paces'. While adjusting to a different lifestyle, the following suggestions may help.

1. *View the change as an opportunity.* This goes back to the High Expectancy Success Theory – the more you expect out of a situation the more you are apt to find. If you can move into a lifestyle transition with a positive attitude, the battle is half-won before you start. The more you sustain your positive focus, the sooner the 'passage' will be over.

2. *Accept the fact that some refocusing will be necessary.* Anticipating adjustments will put you in a better position to take advantage of the eight adjustment techniques presented in Part 2 of this book. You will be more honest with yourself and start the process sooner. Those who expect a difficult transition to be a 'piece of cake' often wind up with egg on their face.

3. *Recognise that temporary letdowns are normal.* Such down periods do not often reach the 'depression stage' where professional help is required. Some work, however, will be necessary on your outlook. Often such letdowns occur after progress has been made and the

individual believes she or he is home and dry. Regaining one's focus during a lifestyle change is similar to getting out of an attitudinal rut.

When I first considered a career in teaching, I was fortunate to have a friend, Dr Willis Kenealy, who made this suggestion: 'If you place more emphasis on keeping a positive attitude than on making money, you will be more successful in your career and the money will take care of itself.' Dr Kenealy was a wise man. He knew that a quest for wealth and attitude have little to do with each other. Like those with lower incomes (who sometimes use a lack of wealth as an excuse to stay negative), the rich don't automatically enjoy a positive attitude. It must be earned through work and practice.

Each individual is free to select his or her most important personal possession. Some select money or other worldly things; others place their highest value on human relationships. Only a few consider personal attitude. This is unfortunate because almost everything starts with a positive attitude.

With a positive attitude you enhance your career (money factor), build better human relationships (happiness factor) and come closer to reaching your life goals. *You win in all directions.*

That is why I honestly believe that *attitude is your most priceless possession!*

Summary

1. Everyone has the capacity to be positive under almost any circumstances.
2. A positive attitude is the key to success in any problem-solving procedure or major lifestyle change.
3. With a consistently positive attitude it is possible to win the game of life in all directions; personal satisfaction, strong relationships and success in a meaningful career.